The Complete Ayurveda Cookbook
for Beginners

Easy and Healthy Ayurveda Diet Recipes to Unlock the Secrets of
Hindu Healing and Live Healthy

By Bob J. Prestin

Table of Content

Introduction

Ayurveda! Today, each time I utter this word, I feel a sense of positivity emanating from my mind and body. The kind of optimistic, confident, healthy, and energic person I am today is all thanks to this ancient Indian system of medicine.

Nowadays, I feel positive, bursting with energy in the morning when I get up, throughout my day at the clinic, and even when I reach home after a tiring day. But life wasn't the same some time back!

I realized it long back that things were taking a worse turn for us, humans. Where are we heading? This thought made me feel nervous and weak. I felt helpless each time I told a young man in his 30s he had diabetes! Sometimes, it was cancer; sometimes, it was a stroke!

That's not done! That's really not done!

We can't let this to happen to ourselves and our next generations. As a doctor, I knew it very well that the primary causes of the declining health status of today's younger generation was a faulty diet, which comprised more of fatty, sugar-laden, junk foods, pollution, radiation from smartphones and mobile towers, stressful lifestyle, sedentary habits and many other things that were in the category of 'undesirable'.

I was desperate to find a solution to the problems we were facing. We couldn't possibly avoid these 'undesirable' factors.

But, then, I found something that could help us avoid the impact of such factors of our life, on our health.

It was Ayurveda!

During my visit to India, I came across this ancient Indian system of holistic healing. And believe me, it changed my life completely.

Ayurveda opened the doors of better health and a better lifestyle for me. I learned how an ayurvedic diet comprised of herbs and spices could protect me against all that was affecting my mind and body adversely.

I had to extend my stay in India so that I could learn more about this science. And after having equipped myself with the concepts of Ayurveda, exercises (called yoga asanas), and a holistic healing diet, I am ready to share all the information with you.

I have been following an ayurvedic diet and lifestyle myself for the past few years. And this is the reason why I feel so young and energetic today! (FYI: I am 50+)

I also saw a drastic improvement in the health of my patients who adopted the ayurvedic lifestyle.

However, I know this is not enough. I want to spread the knowledge of Ayurveda so that men and women in all corners of the world know of this science.

This is why; I decided to write a book about Ayurveda. This book is meant for all young men and women who are at the stage of life where their health is likely to get affected by a stressful lifestyle.

This book is meant for young kids, working professionals, homemakers, businessmen, and all those who would like to improve their health and avoid diseases linked to eating an unhealthy diet, exposure to pollution, radiation, and similar factors.

This book provides information about the principles of Ayurveda, its benefits, healthy lifestyle practices, yoga poses, and medicinal herbs and remedies for common ailments.

And most importantly, I will also share with you some easy-to-prepare recipes made from natural foods, herbs, and spices that will take your health several notches higher!

So, are you ready to go?

Let's begin…

Chapter-1 Ayurveda: An Ancient System of Holistic Healing

Ayurveda! This word resonates a great sense of calmness, spirituality, relaxation, and serenity! Ayurveda is the science of holistic healing that originated in ancient India several centuries ago. It is one of the best and the oldest forms of medical science, the guiding principles, and concepts recommended by which have stood the test of time over several centuries.

According to the modern sources, Ayurveda, as an oral tradition, is believed to have originated between 6,000 to 7,000 BCE. The concepts and principles of this science have been in existence since the period of Indus Valley Civilization.

Ayurveda is a complete science that reveals the real causes responsible for the development of diseases as well as the natural ways to cure them!

Ayurvedic science aims to improve, preserve, and restore health and helps in the management of disorders holistically. It makes use of natural herbal remedies and therapies that are primarily aimed at promoting detoxification, regeneration, and rejuvenation.

Ayurveda offers us a treasure of medicinal compounds and the therapeutic properties hidden within nature in the various compartments of herbs, shrubs, and plants including their roots, flowers, leaves, stem, and even in their barks!

Let us move further to learn more about this ancient science that has the potential to keep you protected against several acute and chronic diseases and improve your lifespan.

An Overview and The Core Concepts of Ayurveda

The word, Ayurveda, is derived from Sanskrit words: Ayur, and Veda. When clubbed together, these words mean, "The knowledge of longevity" (or the ways to improve your lifespan by boosting health and inhibiting diseases).

The wise sages of ancient India had intuitively understood the physical or anatomical structure of the human body. They had also recognized the physiological processes occurring within us related to the healthy functioning of all organs.

They had also conceptualized the relationships between the body, mind, and soul that form a trinity explaining the need to maintain harmony in all the body's organs, mental health, and spirit. Ayurveda describes this through the concept of Tridosha that we will discuss later. Before that, let's have a look at the guiding principles in Ayurveda.

Guiding Principles in Ayurveda

According to Ayurvedic science, every individual is considered a unique individual made up of five primary elements: air, space, fire, water, and earth.

These elements are derived from mother nature. The weather conditions we are exposed to, the food we eat, and environmental factors are some examples of these elements in nature.

An imbalance in these elements produces an adverse influence on us. This theory is explained by the ayurvedic system of medicine through the principle of three doshas and Panchatatva as described beneath:

The Concept of Tridosha and Panchatatva

Ayurveda has put forward the concept of 3 humors called Tridosha that is unique to this healing science.

Ayurveda believes that a human body comprises of 5 universal elements, which are called Panchatatva. These elements include Bhumi (earth), Jala (water), Vayu (air), Akash (space), and Agni (fire). The three doshas are formed from the unique combination of these elements.

Doshas refer to the bio-elements, which determine the constitution or tendencies of any person to develop and prevent certain diseases. It proposes that the healthy functioning of our body as a whole exists only when the balance between these three bio-elements - Vata dosha, Pitta dosha, and Kapha Dosha - is maintained.

These doshas could be roughly translated as Energetic Force.

All the biological, physiological, and metabolic processes occurring in our body, as well as the functions performed by the organs and tissues, depends on the balance between these three doshas. These Tridoshas have also been entrusted with the responsibility to support the sensory functions, movements, transformations, and other activities of our mind and body.

All living beings are born with their own unique balance of these three doshas that together form a specific Prakriti of the person. Prakriti refers to the constitution or disposition that determine any person's fundamental nature and tendencies. It is the Prakriti that plays a crucial role in deciding the illnesses he or she may develop.

If you want to stay healthy and avoid diseases, you must first find the particular dosha that is dominant in your Prakriti. You just need to answer the questions mentioned in the dosha quiz given beneath. This would help you determine the diet you have to follow and other lifestyle changes required to calm the dominant dosha and restore the balance between the three doshas.

Dosha Quiz

1. Body type
a) Thin
b) Medium
c) Large

2. Tendency for weight gain
a) Around the middle
b) Evenly distributed
c) Mainly in rear/thighs

3. Complexion
a) Dark complexion
b) Fair skin
c) Tans evenly

4. Body hair
a) Scanty, curly
b) Light, finely textured
c) Moderate amount of body hair

5. Chin
a) Delicate
b) Moderate
c) Large

6. Hands
a) Cold hands
b) Warm hands
c) Medium temperature

7. Thirst
a) Changeable
b) Excessive
c) Sparse

8. Memory
a) Good short-term memory
b) Quick memory
c) Slow memory

9. Decision making
a) Changes mind easily
b) Quick decisions
c) Slow to make decisions

10. Physical activities
a) Physically active
b) Moderately active
c) Prefers leisurely activities

11. Sleep
a) Light sleeper
b) Sleeps well
c) Heavy sleeper

12. Skin type
a) Dry skin
b) Oily skin
c) Thicker skin

If you answered most questions with the option 'a', you have a Vata Prakriti. If most answers are 'b' and 'c', you have a predominant Pitta and Kapha dosha, respectively.

Why Is The Ancient Science of Ayurveda Perfect for Our Modern Life?

Ayurveda, in spite of being an ancient science of healing, is entirely based on how our mind and body work. The ayurvedic therapies, including herbs and detoxification, have the potential to restore health in various ways.

It is particularly the detoxification therapy, which is referred to as Panchakarma in Ayurveda, that holds special importance in today's world.

Panchakarma therapy forms the crux of treatments of most diseases. This therapy includes 5 actions or five treatment methods, each of which aims to serve a unique purpose to restore your health holistically.

Panchakarma therapy works by balancing the three doshas or humors by restoring the harmony between Panchatatva, the five basic elements in your body, including air, water, fire, earth, and space.

The balance between three doshas is lost due to various factors such as mental stress, pollution in the air, unhealthy fats and sugars in junk foods, additives and preservatives in food, radiation from mobile towers, lack of sleep, and so on.

Today's generation is at grave danger due to the constant exposure to these disease-causing agents. This is where the ancient science of Ayurveda can help us.

Detoxification of the body and cleansing of blood through Panchakarma would protect the cells, tissues, and organs from the impact of these agents and thus prevent diseases.

Panchakarma is particularly recommended when there is an accumulation of harmful toxins in the body. It is a natural cleansing process, which helps to eliminate unwanted toxins from the body. It is a five-fold purification therapy that forms the classical treatment approach in Ayurveda. These specialized procedures comprise of:

- Vaman (Therapeutic emesis or vomiting)
- Nasya (cleansing through the nose)
- Basti (Enema)
- Virechan (Purgation)
- Rakta moksha (Detoxification of the blood through bloodletting)

The panchakarma therapy, in combination with the appropriate dietary and lifestyle changes, Yoga, and meditation, would promote the natural physiological processes in your body, relieve symptoms, and prevent the development and progress of diseases.

Seasonal Adjustments and All-Season Cleanse Panchakarma

Panchakarma is beneficial in all seasons and across all weather conditions. However, this therapy also recommends the use of specific cleansing processes depending on the seasons. The therapy can be modified depending on the weather parameters such as dryness, humidity, and temperature, as well as their effects on the body.

These seasonal adjustments are necessary to cleanse your body thoroughly and optimize the results of Panchakarma.

Does Ayurveda Recommend Any Spiritual Rituals and Practices?

Ayurveda recommends certain rituals and practices that are aimed at improving your overall wellness. These rituals are also meant to improve the connectedness between your mind, body, and soul.

The spiritual practices recommended by Ayurveda include Yoga and Meditation. It also advocates following certain rituals to improve your health as given below:

- Cleaning your tongue using a tongue scraper is considered an excellent way to eliminate bacteria and toxins accumulated in the oral cavity while you are asleep.
- Oil pulling, a practice of using coconut or sesame oil as a mouthwash, is recommended to prevent bad breath and rejuvenate the nerves.
- Self-massage of the body with oil, preferably coconut oil, called abhyanga is an Ayurvedic ritual that produces an amazingly relaxing effect!

Other than these, regular practice of Yoga and meditation is recommended to promote your spiritual well-being and enhance longevity. Let us have a look at the yoga poses that can enhance your health, physically, mentally, and spiritually.

Best Yoga Poses to Improve Your Health

Yoga is an integral part of Ayurveda that is aimed at integrating your mind, body, and soul to boost health. It refers to the union of your soul or inner self with your mind, body, and the universe. .

The Yogis in ancient India believed that a person could stay in harmony with himself and the surroundings if he can integrate his mind, body, and spirit. These three forms of life would be united only when our actions, emotions, and thinking are in balance.

So, the Yogis formulated some ways to help us achieve and maintain this balance. And this is what gave rise to one of the solid foundations of Ayurveda called Yoga.

Yoga exercises, popularly known as yoga poses or asanas, would improve blood circulation in different organs and tissues of the body. They can also stimulate the digestive system and support the endocrinal and glandular functions.

The importance of Yoga in today's world cannot be undermined. We have, nowadays, become accustomed to looking at the outer world only as a source of satisfaction, enjoyment, and fulfillment.

Most of the times, we are striving towards the things, which seem to lie beyond our reach. This is why; we get tangled up in "doing" rather than "being." We are always "in action" without being "aware."

It has become difficult for us to visualize the state of serenity and repose in which our emotions, feelings, and thoughts cease to be restless or in perpetual motion.

Yoga, the ancient spiritual science, would offer direct means for stilling this restlessness of your mind and body. This can halt the natural turbulence of your thoughts that prevent you from knowing what you are.

Yoga would help you realize your integration and oneness with the infinite power, joy, and intelligence thus giving an essence of your inner self.

By allowing you to identify the self-awareness as the fundamental ground of your existence, the practice of Yoga would help you achieve the "union" of your consciousness and soul with the universe.

The primary purpose of Yoga is to feel and attain spiritual enlightenment. If you want to let go of the outward pleasures and find your inner self, you can practice the simple Yoga poses given below:

- Adho Mukha Svanasana
- Setu Bandha Sarv
- Balasana
- Salabhasana
- Shavasana

The spiritual and physical practices recommended by Yoga would support and sustain your overall health and well-being irrespective of your age and fitness. This is why; it is considered a powerful and sophisticated mind-body health system.

Here are some more benefits you will be able to achieve by practicing Yoga:

- Practicing Yoga would help you build a strong and flexible body and encourage a deeper mind-body awareness. The healing would bring about an ability to focus and improve mental clarity in your thoughts.

- Yoga provides you the benefits of exercising in a safe, peaceful, and holistic way. Yoga asanas involve stretching the muscles of different groups, developing abs, biceps, and triceps, toning up the arms and strengthening the back.
- Yoga allows you to notice your breathing pattern by keeping your mind relaxed. This would create a sense of peace within your soul and relax your stressed mind.
- The controlled and repeated breathing pattern during yoga practices would ensure a good supply of oxygen to all the organs of your body.
- Regular practice of Yoga would improve your sleep pattern and help you enjoy a sound sleep.

How Can Medicinal Herbs and Remedies Be Used to Manage Common Ailments?

If we were staying in a perfect world, we would have got all the essential nutrients needed to enhance the functioning of our body simply from the food we consume. However, such a perfect world does not exist!

In fact, today, we are living in a world where there are just too many factors that can harm our health, and these factors far outnumber the factors that support health.

The dangers for our mind, body, and soul include the global warming caused by deforestation and radiation emitted by smartphones. Some other factors, like unchecked industrialization, sedentary habits, stressful life, and the tendency to eat junk foods also affect our health. At the same time, we have lost track of herbs and spices that possess great natural medicinal potential.

If you notice, you would realize most of the factors that are inimical to our health are man-made while the health-boosting factors are natural in origin.

And this is the reason why there is a desperate need to use natural foods in the forms of your diet and herbal remedies to minimize the effect of harmful agents on your body.

Herbs and spices, some of which might be readily available in the spice rack in your kitchen, would help you derive the nature's therapeutic and preventive potential.

These herbs are loaded with excellent medicinal properties. You just need to grab those herbs and use them regularly as an efficient means to stay fit and healthy. Let me reveal some herbal remedies commonly recommended by Ayurveda to avoid illnesses.

- Basil stimulates the appetite and eases stomach upsets. It also supports the kidney functions and detoxifies the blood by eliminating toxins from the body through urine.
- Ginger possesses natural anti-inflammatory properties that would protect your body against infections caused due to bacteria and fungi.
- Cloves are loaded with rich medicinal properties. It acts as a stimulant. It is also rich in iron, sodium, and potassium. It can also be used as a local anesthetic agent for relieving toothache.
- Cinnamon can be used in the management of nutritional deficiencies such as anemia. It can also be used by diabetic patients to manage their blood sugar levels.
- Just a few drops of lavender oil would be sufficient to ignite your senses and help you feel fresh and energetic. It can soothe your stressed mind and irritated nerves at the end of a hectic day.

What Are The Benefits of Ayurveda?

This ancient system of healing from India offers several benefits. And this is why people not just in India, but across the globe are turning to this science to stay healthy. Here are a few benefits of Ayurveda:

- The herbs recommended by Ayurveda offer a mechanism to restore synergy between the body, mind, and soul while supporting your vitality significantly. This is in contrast to the synthetically prepared drugs, which often work by antagonizing the disease processes.

- Unlike the modern system of medicine, Ayurvedic does not recommend a disease-specific approach. It rather aims at determining the characteristics of the internal and external features of the patient to restore and rejuvenate the entire body.

- Since ayurvedic treatments are aimed at identifying and restoring the underlying dosha responsible for disease development, the results of the therapies last longer. This effect of ayurvedic herbs is particularly beneficial for patients diagnosed with chronic ailments like cancer, autoimmune disorders, and allergies.

- Ayurveda emphasizes disease prevention as much as it stresses on disease treatment. Hence, it recommends the use of herbs, detoxification, and other natural therapies even for healthy people. Natural herbs, being restorative and regenerative, help to promote the body's nourishment. They enhance the intellectual and emotional abilities of a person.

- Ayurvedic medications are made from pure and natural herbs. They are devoid of any harmful chemical additives. Therefore, they are less likely to produce any serious side effects.

- The holistic approach adopted during the ayurvedic treatment is aimed at supporting proper absorption, breakdown, and digestion of food. Herbal remedies recommended based on the Prakriti of a person would either decrease or increase the person's appetite depending on his ideal and actual weight.

- The therapeutic potential of Ayurveda would enhance your energy levels and enlighten your soul and mind, thus keeping diseases at bay.

- Herbal remedies recommended by Ayurveda possess high nutritional content and are non-toxic. These herbs offer a source of vitality and energy to your soul and mind besides serving as a substitute for essential nutrients like proteins, vitamins, minerals, and antioxidants needed by your body.

- The plant and mineral-based Ingredients in ayurvedic medications are obtained from natural sources like herbs and rocks, making the entire experience closer to mother nature.

- The ayurvedic system also encompasses the social, intellectual, ethical, and spiritual needs of our life. It encourages mental relaxation, peace, and harmony by recommending effective stress-relieving techniques like Yoga and meditation.

Chapter-2 What Is the Role of Food and Diet in Ayurveda

Ayurveda believes in improving health by natural means, including eating healthy foods. Ayurveda recommends including herbs and spices in our regular diet so that our body can derive the benefits of their medicinal potential.

In fact, diet forms the crux of the concept of holistic healing proposed by Ayurveda. Several centuries ago, when medicinal science we talk about today had not even come into existence, saints and sages in India had devised a healthy diet for humans.

The diet, just as recommended by modern science, provides complete nutrition. It includes all food groups, including the macronutrients like carbohydrates, fats, and proteins and micronutrients like vitamins and minerals.

However, there is much more to the ayurvedic diet than just nutrients. Let us learn more about the role of food and diet in Ayurveda and how it can help improve your health.

The Role of Food in Ayurveda

The dietary habits recommended by Ayurveda is not focused just on providing adequate nutrition to the body. It goes beyond our nutritional needs and encompasses a broader choice of natural sources of food to promote bodily functions.

Ayurvedic diet can be customized based on factors such as the diseases the patient is suffering from or prone to develop as well as the dominant dosha and Prakriti of the person.

Other than these, Ayurveda has also proposed general guidelines that can suit all individuals irrespective of their Prakriti or doshas.

Read on to check how some simple changes in your diet as advised by the ayurvedic science can keep you protected against diseases.

The Six Tastes of Food and Their Importance in the Ayurvedic System of Medicine

We all know there are six basic tastes that our taste buds can recognize. Most foods we eat have a combination of these tastes.

For example; candies are sweet and sour while chips are usually spicy and salty.

It is this mix of different tastes that make the food tempting. Most of us consider taste as just an indication of how delicious the food is.

However, according to Ayurveda, the taste we experience is not just about enjoying the food we eat. Ayurveda goes a step ahead and reveals the meaning each of these tastes can have as far as our health is concerned.

Let's have an Ayurvedic take on the six tastes that goes beyond just pleasing our taste buds.

To begin with, Ayurveda recommends eating a diet that comprises of all six tastes - sweet, salty, sour, bitter, pungent, and astringent. Each meal of the day should include all these tastes to ensure your body receives complete nutrition.

Let me tell you why.

According to Ayurveda, each taste has a specific relationship with your Prakriti and doshas, as explained below:

- The sweet taste, called madhura in Ayurveda, helps to build tissues that are formed from water and earth. Hence, eating sweet foods is believed to strengthen your Kapha dosha.

However, overeating sweets can create an imbalance in the Kapha dosha that must be corrected by consuming foods that have bitter, pungent, and astringent tastes.

- Similarly, sour, salty, and pungent tastes are known to strengthen Pitta dosha. They can help to enhance the functions associated with the rise in your body temperatures, such as metabolic processes and fat burning.

An excess presence of these tastes in your diet, on the other hand, may aggravate Pitta dosha. This can be corrected by balancing out the taste of the foods with sweetish foods.

- Food having bitter, pungent, and astringent tastes tend to increase Vata dosha. These tastes are linked to the body movements, cleansing of channels of excretion and penetration.

If you want to pacify Vata dosha, you need to focus on eating sweet, salty, and sour foods.

The analysis of taste was made by the ancient ayurvedic healers after several centuries of observation. But, it makes as much sense even today. Here's why the link between the specific tastes and their impact on the balance of nutrients and doshas holds higher importance for your diet.

The taste of your food is associated with the chemicals and nutrients your body needs as given below:

- Sweet foods are rich in carbohydrates and contain low to moderate amounts of fats and amino acids.
- Sour foods provide essential organic acids to the body. For example; oranges contain citric acid; apples provide malic acid and yogurt has

lactic acid. Each of these organic acids is required by your body to perform specific functions. A lack of a sour taste in your meals might mean your diet is deficient in these organic acids. Hence, your risk of developing diseases linked to some metabolic processes can increase.

- Needless to say, salty foods contain salts in the forms of minerals like sodium and potassium. Excessive salt in your diet can create an imbalance in the dosha, making you proven to develop hypertension.
- The pungent taste of some foods is due to the volatile oils present in them. These oils produce an encouraging impact on the digestion of food and secretion and release of hormones and enzymes.
- The bitter taste of some vegetables is due to the presence of alkaloids, and glycosides in them and Astringent taste indicate the food contains tannins. Your body needs these nutrients for optimum functioning of the organs.

Due to our busy lifestyle, we hardly get any time to sit comfortably at the dining table and eat foods calmly chewing each bite and relishing the flavors.

What's worse is most of us eat the food while on the run, picking a sandwich from here or a beverage from there. This can prevent us from ensuring you get all the six tastes on your plate in your all meals.

This is why; Ayurveda proposes making healthy changes to your dietary habits. These habits are linked not just to the type of food you eat but also how you eat your meals. It recommends sitting on the floor, if possible, to eat each meal and eating food slowly.

Chewing the food slowly will let all the flavors and tastes to produce their effect on your taste buds. This would not just satisfy your cravings but also ensure your body receives all macronutrients and micronutrients in adequate amounts. The slower you eat the food, the better you will be able to assess whether any taste is lacking.

Your meals should possess a precise blend of all the six tastes. You may modify the flavors by adding spices or seasonings to balance Vata, Pitta and Kapha dosha depending on the disorder you are suffering from or the particular dosha your body is in imbalance.

This is how by simply giving due attention to the taste of the food you eat, you can make sure your body stays in a state of balance and is built to inhibit disease processes.

The Foods You Should Eat

Here are the guidelines about the food to eat and foods to avoid based on your dosha.

Vata dosha

Vata is a dry and cold dosha. Hence, you need to eat warm and nourishing foods having a dense texture. Added butter and fats could be good for stabilizing this dosha. You can choose salty, sweet, and sour tastes and foods that are soothing and satisfying.

Some good options for people with predominant Vata dosha include warm milk, warm soups, cream, butter, stews, hot cereals, raw nuts, freshly baked bread, and nut butter. All sweet fruits are good to eat for people with Vata dosha as long as they are not unripe. The recommend spices include cinnamon, ginger, cloves, cardamom, cumin, and garlic.

People with Vata dosha need to avoid cold foods like salads, iced drinks, and raw vegetables. They should also avoid too much caffeine and unripe fruits as they can disturb Vata.

Pitta dosha

If you belong to the Pitta Prakriti, you can consume foods that are cool or warm and have a moderately heavy texture. However, steaming hot foods must be avoided. Sweet, bitter, and astringent tastes are ideal.

They can eat cool and refreshing foods in summers such as milk, salads, and ice cream.

Pitta dosha can be soothed by drinking herbal tea specifically licorice root and mint tea. Cold cereals, apple tea, and cinnamon toast are good options for breakfast. They should also consume plant-based foods and avoid consuming red meat as it tends to heat the body due to their high-fat content. They should also consume milk, grains, and veggies on a regular basis.

The foods to avoid for people with Pitta dosha includes butter and added fats, sour cream, pickles, and cheese. It is also advisable to use lemon juice instead of vinegar for salad dressing. Coffee, hot, salty, and fermented foods should be avoided.

Kapha dosha

Light, warm, and dry foods are favorable for people with Kapha dosha. The preferred spices are fenugreek, cumin, sesame seed, and turmeric.

They are also advised to eat foods prepared using dry cooking methods such as baking, grilling, broiling, and sautéing. Moist cooking methods like steaming, boiling, and poaching must be avoided.

People with Kapha dosha need to watch out for too many sweets and fats in their meals. They should also limit their salt intake as it can worsen fluid retention. Most people with a Kapha tendency are prone to overeating. Hence, they are advised to eat their main meal in the middle of the day. They can have a dry and light meal in the evening.

If you eat the right foods based on your natural Prakriti and dosha, you would be able to stay in good health, physically as well as mentally, for years after years.

Foods You Must Avoid

Other than the specific foods you must avoid based on your specific dosha, there are certain foods that Ayurveda advises against consuming.

These include:

- Stale food or food that was prepared more than 12 hours ago
- Alcoholic beverages
- An excess of any one form of nutrient or food even if it is supposed to be healthy
- Fruits and vegetables that do not grow naturally in the current season or your geographical locations

What About Meat?

Most people are concerned about whether Ayurveda permits the consumption of meat.

The answer is: Yes, you may eat meat provided you follow certain guidelines. Though Ayurveda advises eating natural foods derived for plant sources, recent years have witnessed a debate about whether meat falls into the criteria of 'healthy foods.'

It is believed that meat could be good for people with Vata dosha. However, if you want to adhere to the Ayurveda dietary guidelines, it is best to avoid meat. If you do want to include it in your diet, make sure it is easier to digest.

You may prepare meat soups that are nourishing and comforting! You can also choose meat of more active animals such as chicken, duck, and goat.

Adaptation of Ayurvedic Principles of A Healthy Diet to A Modern Lifestyle

- Eat natural foods. Avoid genetically-modified or synthetic Ingredients such as chemicals, artificial preservatives, and pesticides in processed foods.
- Eat foods that are closest to nature like fresh whole grains and organically-cultivated fruits and vegetables.
- Shun food fads, drinks, and special diets that are "guaranteed" to work.
- Eat loads of fruits and veggies, not just for their nutritional content but also because they are natural internal cleansers.
- Add spices when necessary. Spices do not just add flavors and aroma to your foods. They also bring great therapeutic value to your meals.
- Avoid eating in the late evening hours as this is the time when the body is ready for rest and hence, not prepared for the processes involved digestion.
- Avoid alcohol, caffeine, and carbonated drinks. Instead, switch to vitality-boosting, life-giving beverages. Begin with water. Drink more water to rehydrate your system and flush out toxins from the body. However, you must avoid drinking ice cold water, especially during and after meals.
- Eat for your soul. Cook and eat meals in a harmonious atmosphere to turn the food into nectar. A tidy, pleasant, and cheerful environment coupled with the nurturing company of family and friends would actually make your mealtimes more nourishing.

5 Tips to Ayurvedic Eating

Other than these, Ayurveda advises people to change the way they eat food. Here are some tips from this ancient Indian system of healing that tell the right ways to eat foods:

1. Sit down on the floor while eating. This posture allows your digestive tract to be positioned in a way that lets you know when you have eaten enough. Sitting down while eating prevents overeating and also supports digestion.
2. Never drink water during meals as it can interfere with the natural processes involved in the breakdown of food. Let the gastric juices act on the food to allow their complete breakdown and assimilation.
3. Always eat freshly cooked meals. Food doesn't taste as great later as it tastes when eaten immediately after it is cooked. Eating foods after several hours of cooking or consuming ready or packaged meals can prevent you from enjoying their natural flavors and keep your cravings dissatisfied.
4. Use slow cooking methods as it prevents the loss of nutrients in the natural sources of foods. This is particularly important for today's generation who prefer to put their ready meals in a microwave oven and consume it.
5. Eat seasonal fruits and veggies as the mother nature knows it better than you what is good for your body during any particular weather.

You Are What You Digest!

Finally, let me make it clear that you are what you can digest. Your digestive health is a reflection of how your body functions. Any disorder or abnormality in any organ or system of your body is bound to reflect in your digestive functions. Hence, if you listen carefully to what your stomach and intestine have to say, you will be able to make the right choices of foods.

If you think your intestine does not agree with certain foods resulting in constipation or loose motions, it indicates an underlying dosha. It necessitates you to avoid that particular food. Similarly, if your stomach feels heavy and bloated after eating certain foods, consider it as a sign that your dominant dosha is aggravated further due to that food.

By listening to these vital cues provided by your stomach and intestine, making healthier changes in your diet can become much easier.

If you follow the dietary habits recommended by Ayurveda, you will find a significant improvement in your health and energy levels. It will restore the balance of three doshas and enhance your mental and physical health significantly.

Ayurvedic Staple and Spices

Ayurvedic diet comprises of several herbs and spices that are known to possess natural medicinal potential. These herbs work on the body to improve the normal physiological process in order to restore health.

Some of the most effective Ayurvedic herbs and spices you can include in your cooking are:

- Turmeric
- Garlic
- Ginger
- Cinnamon
- Tulsi or Holy Basil
- Honey
- Lemon juice

Chapter-3 Ayurvedic Teas and Tonics

Tea To Balance Pitta Dosha

This tea is suitable for people, who suffer from the disorders related to the imbalance in the pitta dosha.

Prep time: 5 minutes, Cook Time: 5 minutes; Serves: 1 (1 cup)

Ingredients

- 1/4 teaspoon coriander
- 1/4 teaspoon fennel
- 1/4 teaspoon cumin seeds
- 1/4 teaspoon fresh cilantro
- 1/4 teaspoon rose petals
- 1 cup of water

Instructions

1. Mix the coriander, fennel, cumin seeds, cilantro, and rose petals.
2. Add a cup of boiling water.
3. Cover the lid and let it steep for five minutes.
4. Strain to discard the herbs and spices and drink lukewarm.

Nutrition Facts Per Serving

Calories 25, Total Fat 0, Saturated Fat 0, Total Carbs 2 to 4 g, Protein 5g, Fiber 3g

Ginger Tea

Suitable for relieving cold, cough, and fever. Soothes the sore throat and heals stomach ailments.

Prep time: 5 minutes, cook time: 10 minutes; Serves 1

Ingredients

- 1 cup of water
- 3-inch strip orange peel
- 1 tsp ginger root, grated
- 2 cloves
- 1 1/ 2 tsp honey
- 1-inch piece cinnamon bark

Instructions

1. Bring water to a boil.
2. Add in all other Ingredients, and bring the heat down to medium.
3. Let it steep for about ten to fifteen minutes.
4. Strain into a mug and drink while it is warm.

Nutrition Facts Per Serving

Calories 35, Total Fat 0, Saturated Fat 0, Total Carbs 2 to 3 g, Protein 4g, Fiber 1 to 2 g.

Cumin, Coriander, and Fennel Tea

Supports digestion and eases constipation, bloating, and heaviness in the stomach.

Prep time: 5 minutes, cook time: 10 minutes; Serves1

Ingredients

- A cup of water
- 1/4 tsp cumin seeds
- 1/4 tsp coriander seeds
- 1/4 tsp fennel seeds

Instructions

1. Boil 1 cup of water
2. Add the whole cumin, coriander seeds, and fennel seeds.
3. Let it steep for 5 minutes
4. Strain to discard the spices and serve hot.

Nutrition Facts Per Serving

Calories 15, Total Fat 0, Saturated Fat 0, Total Carbs 1 to 2 g, Protein 1 to 2 g, Fiber 0 to 1 g.

Lemon Weight Loss Tea

Drink in the morning after breakfast, or between meals to quench hunger and stimulate fat burning.

Prep time: 5 minutes, cook time: 0 minutes; Serves 1

- 1/4 whole lemon

- A cup of water

- 2 pinches of apple cider vinegar

- 1 pinch cayenne pepper

- 1 tsp honey

1. Squeeze lemon into hot water and stir.
2. Add remaining Ingredients and stir well.
3. Drink immediately

Calories 10, Total Fat 0, Saturated Fat 0, Total Carbs 2 g, Protein 1 g, Fiber 0 to 1 g.

Vata Balancing Tea with Cardamom and Ginger

Suitable for balancing Vata dosha. It can correct the imbalance of Vata dosha and provide relief from the symptoms such as joint pains when consumed on a regular basis.

Prep time: 5 minutes, cook time: 0 minutes; Serves 1

Ingredients

- A cup of water
- 1/4 tsp sugar
- 2 pinch cardamom powder
- 1/4-inch fresh ginger, finely grated
- 1/4 whole lime

Instructions

1. Boil water.
2. Add other Ingredients and let it steep 3 to 5 minutes.
3. Strain to remove herbs and drink it warm.

Nutrition Facts Per Serving

Calories 16, Total Fat 0, Saturated Fat 0, Total Carbs 2 g, Protein 1 g, Fiber 1g.

Pepper and Lemon Tea

Consume lemon pepper tea regularly to boost your immunity and avoid recurrent attacks of allergies. It can also reduce the tendency to catch cold and other infections.

Prep time: 5 minutes, cook time: 0 minutes; Serves 1

Ingredients

- Juice of 1 lemon
- 1/2 tsp turmeric
- 1/4 tsp black pepper powder
- A cup of boiling water
- 1 1/2 tsp honey
- ½ tsp lemon juice

Instructions

1. Place turmeric and pepper in a cup
2. Pour boiling water over it.
3. Stir in the honey and lemon juice and drink immediately

Nutrition Facts Per Serving

Calories 19, Total Fat 0, Saturated Fat 0, Total Carbs 4, Fiber 2 g.

Tulsi Tea

Drink this tea regularly if you have a tendency to develop skin problems like acne breakouts. It is also good for boosting immunity.

Prep time: 5 minutes, cook time: 10 minutes; Serves 1

Ingredients

- 1/4 cup basil
- One and a quarter cup of water
- 2 tsp lemon juice
- 1 tsp honey

Instructions

1. Place basil leaves in a saucepan. Add one and a quarter cup of water. Bring to a boil.
2. Lower the flame and allow to steep for another 10 minutes.
3. Strain into a cup. Add the lemon juice and honey.
4. Stir well and drink warm.

Nutrition Facts Per Serving

Calories 18, Total Fat 0, Saturated Fat 0, Total Carbs 3 g, Protein 2 g, Fiber 1 g.

Mint Tea

Mint tea helps to improve memory and increase energy levels. It can refresh your senses ad help you fight fatigue.

Prep time: 5 minutes, cook time: 10 minutes; Serves 1

Ingredients

- 10 to 12 mint leaves
- A cup of water
- 1 sprig rosemary
- A squeeze lemon, optional

Instructions

1. Tear and crush the mint leaves and place them into a cup.
2. Boil water. Plop rosemary in the pan.
3. Pour it over the mint leaves in the cup. Close the lid and let it sit for 10 minutes.
4. Squeeze in lemon juice and drink immediately.

Nutrition Facts Per Serving

Calories 14, Total Fat 0, Saturated Fat 0, Total Carbs 3 to 4 g, Protein 1 or 2 g, Fiber 1 g.

Chapter-4 Breakfast Recipes

Cream of Rice Soup with Garlic Cilantro, and Ginger

Eat a bowl of rice for your breakfast. The glycemic index of this recipe is suitable to maintain stable blood sugar levels. It will keep you feeling fuller until the lunchtime thus controlling your food intake.

Prep time: 10 minutes, cook time: 10 minutes; Serves 4

Ingredients

- 1 cup of rice
- 1 clove of garlic
- ½-inch ginger, grated
- 1 tbsp olive oil

- 2 cups of water
- 1/4 cup chopped cilantro
- 2 pinch black pepper powder
- 1/4 tsp salt

Instructions

1. Grind the rice grains in a coffee grinder.
2. Chop garlic and ginger. Fry them in olive oil in a saucepan.
3. Add 2 cups water. Bring to a boil.
4. Add remaining Ingredients and keep stirring for a few minutes.
5. Reduce heat to low and let it simmer for another ten minutes or until the rice is cooked properly.

Nutrition Facts Per Serving

Calories 170, Total Fat 10 g, Total Carbs 50 to 60 g, Protein 25 g, Fiber 25 g.

Roasted Rice with Cinnamon Dates, and Cardamom

Eating a bowl of rice for your breakfast will provide a surge of energy to help you perform your routine activities with better ease.

Prep time: 5 minutes, cook time: 25 minutes; Serves 4

Ingredients

- 4 dates, dried
- 1 tbsp olive oil
- 1 cup of rice
- 1/4 tsp black pepper powder
- 1/4 tsp cinnamon powder
- 1/4 tsp cardamom powder
- 2 pinch salt
- 3 cups of water

Instructions

1. Chop dates to make tiny pieces.
2. Heat a medium saucepan and add olive oil. Once it melts, add rice grains.
3. Stir for 2 to 5 minutes, until all the rice is coated with olive oil.
4. Add dates, spices, and salt. Stir well for a minute.
5. Add water and bring to a boil.
6. Cover the pot and lower the heat.
7. Cook until rice is cooked.

Nutrition Facts Per Serving

Calories 190, Total Fat 12 g, Total Carbs 60 to 80 g, Protein 30 g, Fiber 25 g.

Cinnamon Oatmeal with Almonds & Milk

Suitable especially for people who prefer a high protein diet to support their workout regime.

Prep time: 10 minutes, cook time: 10 minutes; Serves 1

Ingredients

- 2 tbsp almonds
- 1/3 cup of oatmeal or oats
- 1/4 tsp cardamom powder
- 1/4 tsp cinnamon powder
- 1 tsp olive oil
- 1 tsp maple syrup
- 1 cup of milk

Instructions

1. Soak the almonds the previous night. Peel them gently in the morning.
2. Blend the almonds and oatmeal in a coffee grinder.
3. Place this oatmeal mix in a pot. Add the remaining Ingredients. You may increase or decrease the quantity of the milk depending on how thick or watery you would like the dish to be.
4. Bring to a boil while stirring constantly.
5. Lower the heat to a simmer and continue cooking until oats become soft.
6. Serve immediately

Nutrition Facts Per Serving

Calories 190, Total Fat 10 g, Total Carbs 40 g, Protein 30g, Fiber 13 g.

Baked Pear and Cardamom

The rich nutritional content of avocado would support your body's natural functions and restore health.

Prep time: 5 minutes, cook time: 10 minutes; Serves 2

Ingredients

- 1/2 cup of water
- 2 pears, medium-sized
- 1/2 tsp cardamom powder

Instructions

1. Preheat the oven to 350 degrees F.
2. Make a thin coating at the bottom of the dish using water.
3. Lay the whole pears on a baking dish.
4. Sprinkle cardamom powder on the pears.
5. Bake at 350 degrees F until they become tender.

Nutrition Facts Per Serving

Calories 60, Total Fat 20 g, Total Carbs 20 g, Protein 25 g, Fiber 8 g.

Grapefruit with Ginger and Honey

This recipe is suitable for people on a keto diet. The natural sweetener, honey, added to it would satisfy their craving for carbs while limiting their total carbohydrate intake.

Prep time: 5 minutes, cook time: 0 minutes; Serves 1

Ingredients

- 1 cup of grapefruit, sliced
- 2 pinches cardamom powder
- 2 pinches dried ginger powder
- 1 tsp honey

Instructions

1. Peel grapefruit and slice it in flat circles.
2. Mix cardamom, ginger, and honey to make a paste. Drizzle it over the grapefruit slices.

Nutrition Facts Per Serving

Calories 40, Total Fat 8 g, Total Carbs 12 g, Protein 10 g, Fiber 7 g.

Roasted Coconut Oatmeal

This is a perfect recipe for keto dieters who would like to stimulate ketosis. The MCTs or medium-chain triglycerides in coconut oil will support the ketone body production and help them get into ketosis faster.

Prep time: 10 minutes, cook time: 15 minutes; Serves 3

Ingredients

- 3 cups of water
- 1 tsp sugar
- 1 tbsp coconut oil
- 1 cup oatmeal or oats
- 3 tbsp coconut flakes
- 3 tbsp sesame seeds
- 2 pinch salt

Instructions

1. Bring water to a boil, and add the sugar and oil. Let it simmer for a few minutes.
2. Meanwhile, grind the oatmeal in a grinder.
3. Roast the coconut flakes and sesame seeds on medium heat until they become light brown.
4. Mix the oatmeal in a cup of water. Add salt.
5. Add oatmeal to the boiling water. Continue boiling while stirring constantly.
6. Let is cook until it becomes soft and has a creamy consistency. Garnish with roasted sesame seeds and coconut flakes.

Nutrition Facts Per Serving

Calories 180, Total Fat 35 g, Total Carbs 35 g, Protein 20 g, Fiber 10 g.

Ginger And Apple Sauce

The goodness of ginger and apples would support your digestion and relieve heaviness in the stomach and bloating. A perfect recipe to try for your breakfast when you have had a heavy dinner the previous night.

Prep time: 10 minutes, cook time: 10 minutes; Serves 1

Ingredients

- 1 cups of grated apple
- ½ cup of water
- 1 tbsp sugar
- 1/4 tsp ginger, dried

Instructions

1. Peel the apples and remove the core. Thinly slice it into tiny pieces.
2. Place the pieces in a saucepan. Add water and let it simmer until the apples become tender.
3. Add sugar and dry ginger and bring to a simmer while stirring occasionally.
4. Serve warm.

Nutrition Facts Per Serving

Calories 50, Total Fat 19 g, Total Carbs 25 g, Protein 10 g, Fiber 10 g.

Quinoa, Date and Walnut Cereal

Dates and walnuts are rich in proteins while quinoa has a high fiber content. This would keep you feeling full for a longer duration and support the body's healing processes.

Prep time: 5 minutes, cook time: 30 minutes; Serves 2

Ingredients

- 1/4 cup walnuts
- 3 whole dates
- 1/2 cup Quinoa
- 1/4 tsp salt
- A cup of water
- 1 tsp maple syrup

Instructions

1. Chop walnuts and dry roast them in a medium saucepan on medium heat until they become brown.
2. Meanwhile, chop dates.
3. Add quinoa, dates, and salt to the pan. Continue frying for another one or two minutes.
4. Add water and bring it to a boil.
5. Lower the heat and cover the lid. Continue simmering for another 20 minutes or until quinoa becomes soft.
6. Add maple syrup and serve.

Nutrition Facts Per Serving

Calories 190, Total Fat 29 g, Total Carbs 31 g, Protein 10g, Fiber 13g.

Chapter-5 Ayurvedic Lunch Recipes

Mung Dal and Coconut Kitchari

Suitable for people who suffer from aggravated Pitta dosha.

Prep time: 10 minutes, cook time: 60 minutes; Serves 4

Ingredients

- 1 cup of rice
- 1/2 cup Mung beans
- 3/4-inch ginger
- 1/3 cup chopped cilantro
- 1/3 cup coconut flakes
- 6 cups of water
- 2 tbsp olive oil
- 1/4 tsp salt
- 1/2 tsp turmeric

Instructions

1. Wash rice and mung dal separately. Soak mung beans for 4 hours.
2. Put ginger, cilantro, coconut flakes, and one cup of water into a food processor. Blend until liquefied.
3. Heat olive oil on medium heat in a saucepan. Add the blended items, salt, and turmeric. Bring to a boil while stirring well.
4. Mix in the mung beans, rice, and five cups of water. Boil for five minutes.
5. Turn down the heat and simmer for 25 to 30 minutes or until the rice and dal are cooked.

Nutrition Facts Per Serving

Calories 210, Total Fat 40 g, Total Carbs 45 g, Protein 30 g, Fiber 15 g.

Sweet Potatoes with Kale

Suitable for all people, including those with diabetes. The complex carbs would keep the carbohydrate metabolism balanced and prevent spikes in blood glucose levels.

Prep time: 15 minutes, cook time: 25 minutes; Serves 2

Ingredients

- 1/2 lbs kale

- 2 cups sweet potato, cubed

- A cup of water

- 2 pinch salt

- 3/4-inch fresh ginger

- 1 tbsp olive oil

Instructions

1. Boil kale until the leaves turn green. Strain the leaves.
2. Add diced sweet potatoes in a separate pot with water just enough to cover them.
3. Add salt and boil until potatoes become soft.
4. Take another pan. Grate and sauté ginger in olive oil for 20 to 30 seconds. Add to it cooked sweet potato and kale. Mix gently and serve.

Nutrition Facts Per Serving

Calories 70, Total Fat 20 g, Total Carbs 25 g, Protein 18 g, Fiber 9 g.

Mung Dal Kitchari

Suitable for relieving symptoms caused due to the imbalance in Vata dosha.

Prep time: 10 minutes, cook time: 60 minutes; Serves 4

Ingredients

- 1/2 cup mung beans
- 4 cups of water
- 1-inch fresh ginger
- 1 tsp cumin
- 1/4 tsp asafoetida
- 1/4 tsp Ajwain

- 1/2 tsp turmeric
- 1/2 tsp salt
- 2 tbsp olive oil
- 1 tsp mustard seeds
- 1 cup of rice

Instructions

1. Soak mung beans for 4 hours and drain. Bring mung beans and water to a boil. Strain out the liquid.
2. Meanwhile, grate and mash the piece of ginger with a mortar and pestle.
3. Set mustard seeds aside. Mix the remaining Ingredients together and make a thick paste by adding one tsp water.
4. Fry mustard seeds in olive oil until they start popping.
5. Add the paste of spices, and fry for another thirty seconds.
6. Add this mixture to mung bean.
7. Continue to simmer for an hour.
8. When mung beans soften, add rice and one more cup of water. Cook until tender.

Nutrition Facts Per Serving

Calories 250, Total Fat 40 g, Total Carbs 50 g, Protein 32g, Fiber 22 g.

Carrot and Kale Soup

A warm and filling lunch with this soup would refresh your energy levels and increase your alertness levels.

Prep time: 10 minutes, cook time: 40 minutes; Serves 4

Ingredients

- 4 whole carrots
- 1/2 tsp fennel seeds
- 1-inch fresh ginger
- 1/2 lbs kale
- 1/4 whole lime
- 1/2 tsp salt
- 1 tbsp olive oil

Instructions

1. Chop carrots and kale and place them in a pot.
2. Add water until the vegetables are covered.
3. Boil the Ingredients until kale becomes soft. Serve warm.

Nutrition Facts Per Serving

Calories 50, Total Fat 12 g, Total Carbs 8 g, Protein 8 g, Fiber 3 g.

Chickpea Khichari

This Khichari is high on spices and flavors. It would satisfy your cravings for delicious food without affecting your efforts to lose weight. A perfect recipe to try on a cheat day while on a weight loss or keto diet.

Prep time: 10 minutes, cook time: 60 minutes; Serves 4

Ingredients

- 1/2 cup chickpeas
- 10 cups of water
- 1-inch fresh ginger
- 1/4 tsp cloves
- 1/2 tsp cinnamon powder
- 1 cup of rice
- 4 bay leaves
- 1/4 tsp salt

Instructions

1. Soak chickpeas overnight and drain the water. Add 6 cups of water and bring to a boil.
2. Strain out the liquid. Add another 4 cups of water and boil again. Add ginger, cloves, and cinnamon. Cook for 40 to 50 minutes.
3. Add rice and the remaining Ingredients. Stir well. Cover the lid and cook on medium heat for 20 to 25 minutes.

Nutrition Facts Per Serving

Calories 240, Total Fat 35 g, Total Carbs 45 g, Protein 35 g, Fiber 18 g.

Butternut Squash Soup

Soothes irritated throat and relieves nasal congestion. Suitable in winter months when you would like to overcome feeling frozen.

Prep time: 20 minutes, cook time: 30 minutes; Serves 4

Ingredients

- 4 cup butternut squash
- 2 tbsp olive oil
- 1/2 cup yellow onion, chopped
- 1/2-inch ginger
- 2 cloves of garlic
- 1/4 tsp black pepper
- 1/4 tsp salt
- 1 tsp fennel seeds
- 4 cups of water
- 1/2 whole lime

Instructions

1. Roast butternut squash in the oven at 350 degrees F for 20 to 30 minutes. Let it cool. Remove the skin. Chop the butternut squash into small cubes.
2. Heat olive oil in a large pot. Add chopped onions and sauté. Add chopped ginger and garlic.
3. Add pepper, salt, and fennel seeds. Fry for another 30 seconds making sure not to burn the seeds and garlic.
4. Add cubes of butternut squash, and water. Bring to a boil.
5. Reduce the heat and cook for 20 minutes. Mash with a potato masher. Squeeze in the juice of a lime and serve hot with a hunk of bread!

Nutrition Facts Per Serving

Calories 170, Total Fat 28 g, Total Carbs 35 g, Protein 20 g, Fiber 17 g.

Potato Latkes

Prep time: 20 minutes, cook time: 10 minutes; Serves 2

Ingredients

- 4 potatoes
- 1/4 cup shallots
- 2 tbsp spelt flour
- 2 eggs
- 1/2 tsp salt
- 1/2 tsp black pepper
- 1/4 cup olive oil

Instructions

1. Grate potatoes using a cheese grater. Add chopped shallots, flour, eggs, salt, and pepper.
2. Add olive oil in a large frying pan. Pout scoops of potato mix to make pancakes about 3 inches in diameter.
3. Let each pancake fry for 3 to 4 minutes on one side and then, flip.
4. Serve immediately with apple sauce or cottage cheese.

Nutrition Facts Per Serving

Calories 60, Total Fat 25 g, Total Carbs 30 g, Protein 22 g, Fiber 14 g.

Quinoa with Red Onion

Prep time: 10 minutes, cook time: 30 minutes; Serves 4

Ingredients

- 1 cup quinoa
- 1/4 cup red onion, chopped
- 1 cup chopped cilantro
- 1/4 tsp black pepper
- 2 tbsp mint leaves
- 1 tsp salt

Instructions

1. Boil quinoa in water for 15 minutes. Finely chop onions and mint and add to quinoa.
2. Mix all other Ingredients.
3. Serve immediately.

Nutrition Facts Per Serving

Calories 180, Total Fat 34 g, Total Carbs 38 g, Protein 20 g, Fiber 18 g.

Chapter-6 Ayurvedic Recipes for Dinner

Asparagus Risotto

Suitable for supporting weight loss. The dietary fibers in this dish would keep your cravings and appetite in control and help you follow a low-calorie diet.

Prep time: 15 minutes, cook time: 40 minutes; Serves 4

Ingredients

- 2 pinch saffron strands
- 2 cups of water
- 2 cups asparagus
- 1 tsp cumin
- 2 tbs olive oil
- 1 cup Risotto
- 1/4 tsp black pepper
- 1/2 tsp salt

Instructions

1. Add a few drops of water in a bowl and let saffron strands soak into it.
2. Meanwhile, bring 1 cup of water to a boil in a pan and set aside.
3. Dice asparagus.
4. Sauté cumin seeds in olive oil in a pot. Add asparagus, risotto, and other Ingredients. Sauté for 30 seconds.
5. Add 1 cup of boiling water and lower the heat. Let is simmer for about 10 minutes and serve immediately.

Nutrition Facts Per Serving

Calories 109, Total Fat 20 g, Total Carbs 38 g, Protein 12 g, Fiber 19 g.

Coconut Rice

This is a perfect recipe for keto dieters who would like to stimulate ketosis. The MCTs or medium-chain triglycerides in coconut oil would support ketone body production and help them get into ketosis faster.

Prep time: 5 minutes, cook time: 25 minutes; Serves 4

Ingredients

- 3 cups of water
- 1 cup of rice
- 1/4 tsp salt
- 2 tbsp coconut oil
- 1/2 cup coconut flakes

Instructions

1. Bring water to a boil and add rice.
2. Add salt, coconut oil, and half of the coconut flakes. Lower the heat and allow to simmer. Cook until rice becomes tender.
3. Meanwhile, roast the remaining coconut flakes. Garnish the flakes over rice and serve.

Nutrition Facts Per Serving

Calories 170, Total Fat 35 g, Total Carbs 35 g, Protein 20 g, Fiber 10 g.

Potato Leek Soup

Soothes sore throat and relieves congestion in the chest and nose. Suitable in winter months to warm up the body.

Prep time: 10 minutes, cook time: 45 minutes; Serves 4

Ingredients

- 6 cups of water
- 4 whole potatoes
- 1 cup leeks
- 1 tbsp fennel seeds
- 1/2 tsp salt
- 1 tsp black pepper
- 2 pinch red pepper flakes

Instructions

1. Heat 4 cups of water. Meanwhile, peel potatoes and chop them into about 1-inch cubes. Add them to the water and bring to a boil.
2. Strain the potatoes after boiling for about 10 minutes.
3. Then, slice the leeks into small pieces.
4. Blend potatoes along with leeks. Add to a pan and bring to a boil with 2 cups of water.
5. Add the remaining Ingredients and heat for another twenty minutes.
6. Garnish with pepper and red pepper flakes and serve hot.

Nutrition Facts Per Serving

Calories 172, Total Fat 28 g, Total Carbs 39 g, Protein 20 g, Fiber 17 g.

Lemon Rice

Eating a bowl of lemon rice for your lunch would keep your blood sugar levels stable. The glycemic index of this recipe is suitable to control diabetes. It would also keep you feeling full thus controlling your total daily food intake.

Prep time: 10 minutes, cook time: 60 minutes; Serves 4

Ingredients

- 1/2 tsp cumin
- 1/2 tsp mustard seeds
- 1/2 cup cashew
- 1 cup of rice
- 1/4 cup olive oil

- 2 cups of water
- 1/2 tsp salt
- 1/2 tsp turmeric
- 1 cup peas
- 2 whole lemons

Instructions

1. Dry roast cumin and mustard seeds.
2. In a separate pot, roast cashews and rice in olive oil.
3. Add 2 cups of water and spices. bring to a boil, cover the lid, and simmer for 25 minutes.
4. Add peas and continue simmering for 10 minutes.
5. Squeeze in lemon juice over the rice and serve hot.

Nutrition Facts Per Serving

Calories 170, Total Fat 12 g, Total Carbs 50 to 60 g, Protein 26 g, Fiber 25 g.

Cabbage Soup

A perfect recipe for weight watchers. Drinking this warm soup would increase your energy levels without adding in too many calories to your diet.

Prep time: 10 minutes, cook time: 30 minutes; Serves 4

Ingredients

- 1/4 tsp black pepper
- 4 cup shredded cabbage
- 1/4 cup celery stalk
- 1 clove garlic
- 1/4 cups chopped parsley
- 1/2 tsp salt
- 1/4 cup yellow onion

Instructions

1. Add all Ingredients in a large pot. Add water enough to cover the vegetables.
2. Then, bring it to a boil. Reduce heat to a simmer.
3. Cook for 20 minutes and serve hot.

Nutrition Facts Per Serving

Calories 50, Total Fat 13 g, Total Carbs 6 g, Protein 8 g, Fiber 3 g.

Coconut and Cilantro Pancake

Suitable for keto dieters to kickstart ketosis and lose weight more easily.

Prep time: 5 minutes, cook time: 15 minutes; Serves 2

Ingredients

- 1/4 cup rice
- 1/4 cup mung beans
- 4 cups of water
- 1/4 tsp salt
- 1 tbsp coconut oil
- 1/4 tsp black pepper
- 1/4 cilantro
- 1/4 cup coconut flakes

Instructions

1. Soak rice and mung bean in water for two hours. Grind together to make a thick batter. Add salt.
2. Heat a large frying pan and add coconut oil. Once it melts, pour 1 cup of the batter onto the pan to make fluffy pancakes.
3. Let it cook on one side and then, flip it to cook the other side.
4. Remove and garnish with black pepper, cilantro, and coconut flakes.

Nutrition Facts Per Serving

Calories 60, Total Fat 22 g, Total Carbs 30 g, Protein 22 g, Fiber 11 g.

Chickpea with Coconut Pesto

This dish would satisfy your cravings for spicy food. A perfect recipe you can try on a cheat day while on a keto diet.

Prep time: 10 minutes, cook time: 10 minutes; Serves 4

- 1 cup chickpeas
- 1 tbsp olive oil
- 1/2 cup coconut milk
- 1/2 cup basil
- 1/4 tsp salt
- 1/2 whole lime

Instructions

1. Soak chickpeas for 4 hours in enough water.
2. Whisk together the lime juice and coconut milk in a medium-sized bowl until the consistency becomes smooth.
3. Finely chop the stem of basil on a cutting board.
4. Puree the basil and salt in a food processor. Set aside the pesto to marinate the flavors.
5. Drizzle olive oil on a frying pan.
6. Strain the chickpeas. Add them to the pan and sauté until they are browned and crispy.
7. Pour the sauce and mix with the chickpeas. Squeeze in the lemon juice.

Nutrition Facts Per Serving

Calories 240, Total Fat 36 g, Total Carbs 42 g, Protein 35 g, Fiber 18 g.

Potatoes with Roasted Sesame

This recipe is suitable for people on a keto diet. Healthy fats in coconut and sesame seeds would stimulate ketosis.

Prep time: 10 minutes, cook time: 10 minutes; Serves 4

Ingredients

- 2 whole potatoes
- 3 tbsp coconut flakes
- 3 tbsp sesame seeds
- 2 pinch salt
- 1 whole lime

Instructions

1. Boil the potatoes in enough water.
2. Meanwhile, roast the coconut flakes and sesame seeds until browned. Once the potatoes are cooked, strain them. Smash them and add salt.
3. Drizzle lime juice on the potatoes and mix in sesame seeds and coconut.

Nutrition Facts Per Serving

Calories 60, Total Fat 8 g, Total Carbs 25 g, Protein 10 g, Fiber 13 g.

Carrots with Lemon and Honey

A healthy and quick weight loss recipe you can try on days you are too tired to spend hours in the kitchen.

Prep time: 4 minutes, cook time: 10 minutes; Serves 2

Ingredients

- 1/8-inch ginger
- 3 whole carrots
- 1/4 whole lemon
- 1 tsp honey
- 1 pinch salt

Instructions

1. Finely chop the ginger.
2. Then, steam the ginger and carrots until tender. Put in a small bowl.
3. Add the juice the lemon, honey, and salt in a bowl and mix well.
4. Drizzle this mixture over the carrots.

Nutrition Facts Per Serving

Calories 49, Total Fat 8 g, Total Carbs 12 g, Protein 10 g, Fiber 7 g.

Collard Greens with Turmeric

Suitable for people with iron deficiency anemia. Also good for pregnant and breastfeeding women in whom the body's iron requirement is higher.

Prep time: 15 minutes, cook time: 30 minutes; Serves 4

Ingredients

- 2 lbs collard greens
- 1 whole potato
- 2 pinch black pepper
- 1/4 whole lemon
- 1 tsp olive oil
- 1 pinch salt
- 2 pinch turmeric
- 1 cup of water

Instructions

1. Finely chop collard greens. Dice the potato.
2. Add ground black pepper, juice of lemon, and the remaining Ingredients in a cup of water and bring it to a boil.
3. Lower the heat and simmer until potatoes are cooked and collard greens have become tender.

Nutrition Facts Per Serving

Calories 89, Total Fat 24 g, Total Carbs 31 g, Protein 12 g, Fiber 13 g.

Chapter-7 Ayurvedic Recipes for Desserts

Almond Date Shake

A yummy treat you can have after dinner or even in the evening. Suitable for weight loss as it does not contain simple carbohydrates.

Prep time: 5 minutes, cook time: 0 minutes; Serves 1

Ingredients

- 2 dates
- 1 cup almond milk
- 2 pinch cinnamon
- 1/8-inch ginger

Instructions

1. Remove the seed from the dates.
2. Warm almond milk in advance, and allow to cool.
3. Puree all Ingredients together in a blender. Drink immediately or chilled.

Nutrition Facts Per Serving

Calories 89, Total Fat 25 g, Total Carbs 35 g, Protein 19 g, Fiber 18 g.

Roasted Rice with Cinnamon and Dates

This recipe can also double up as your main menu for dinner if you are looking to satisfy your craving for desserts.

Prep time: 5 minutes, cook time: 25 minutes; Serves 4

Ingredients

- 4 whole dates
- 1 tbsp Ghee
- 1 cup of rice
- 1/4 tsp black pepper
- 1/4 tsp cardamom
- 1/4 tsp cinnamon
- 2 pinch salt
- 3 cups of water

Instructions

1. Chop dates.
2. Heat a saucepan, and add ghee. Once it melts, add rice grains. Stir for 2 to 5 minutes, until the rice is coated with ghee.
3. Add dates and spices. Stir for one or two minutes.
4. Add water and bring it to a boil. Cover the lid and cook until rice is tender.

Nutrition Facts Per Serving

Calories 149, Total Fat 30 g, Total Carbs 41 g, Protein 10 g, Fiber 10 g.

Peppermint Cocoa Shake

Reserve this recipe for cheat days on a weight loss or a keto diet as it contains a comparatively higher amount of carbs and calories.

Prep time: 5 minutes, cook time: 5 minutes; Serves 1

Ingredients

- 1/2 cup banana chunks
- 2 whole dates
- 1/4 tsp cardamom
- 3/4 cup almond milk
- 1/4 tsp peppermint leaves
- 1 tbsp chocolate or cacao

Instructions

1. Chop 1 whole banana, dates, and combine with cardamom, almond milk, peppermint leaves, and cacao in a blender.
2. Blend until smooth.
3. Serve chilled or at room temperature. You may garnish it with a crushed candy cane.

Nutrition Facts Per Serving

Calories 139, Total Fat 44 g, Total Carbs 51 g, Protein 25 g, Fiber 23 g.

Banana Smoothie with Cardamom

A quick and refreshing recipe. Can have it as many times as you feel like in a day as it contains less number of calories.

Prep time: 5 minutes, cook time: 0 minutes; Serves 1

Ingredients

- 1/3 whole lime
- 2 cup banana chunks
- 1/4 tsp cardamom
- 1 cup of coconut water

Instructions

1. Juice the lime.
2. Combine all Ingredients and add to a blender. Puree until smooth.
3. Serve chilled.

Nutrition Facts Per Serving

Calories 49, Total Fat 10 g, Total Carbs 13 g, Protein 8 g, Fiber6 g.

Banana with Cinnamon

Easy to prepare recipe for keto dieters.

Prep time: 5 minutes, cook time: 0 minutes; Serves1

Ingredients

- 1 cup banana chunks
- 1 tsp ghee
- 2 pinch cinnamon
- 2 pinch ginger

Instructions

1. Deep fry the bananas chunks in ghee. Or, sauté bananas chunks in ghee while tossing them gently.
2. Garnish with spices.

Nutrition Facts Per Serving

Calories 48, Total Fat 21 g, Total Carbs 22 g, Protein 10 g, Fiber 12 g.

Almond Coconut Fudge

Very easy to prepare recipe that is perfect for keto dieters for its low carb content.

Prep time: 5 minutes, cook time: 0 minutes; Serves 1

Ingredients

- 1/4 tsp cinnamon
- 1/4 tsp ginger
- /4 cup almond butter
- 1 tbsp honey

Instructions

1. Use dried, and powdered cinnamon and ginger.
2. Place all the Ingredients in a bowl. Mash together until mixed well.
3. Refrigerate for half an hour and serve chilled.

Nutrition Facts Per Serving

Calories 58, Total Fat 18 g, Total Carbs 20 g, Protein 10 g, Fiber 10 g.

Baked peaches with Vanilla, and Nutmeg

The high fiber content of peaches and the calming effect of nutmeg make this recipe great for relieving digestive problems as well as sleep disturbances.

Prep time: 5 minutes, cook time: 60 minutes; Serves 4

Ingredients

- 4 whole peaches
- 1/4 tsp cloves
- 1/4 tsp nutmeg
- 1 tsp sugar
- 1 tsp vanilla extract
- A cup of water

Instructions

1. Slice peaches in halves and remove the pit.
2. Mix spices, sugar, and vanilla extract with 1 cup of water in a medium bowl. Pour this mixture over peaches.
3. Bake at 325 degrees F for one hour.

Nutrition Facts Per Serving

Calories 119, Total Fat 24 g, Total Carbs 32 g, Protein 12 g, Fiber 20 g.

Honey and Spice Throat Coat

This syrup should be savored and licked from a spoon. The honey would coat the back of your throat with the spices. The spices are highly effective for relieving sore throat, runny noses, and flu-like symptoms.

Prep time: 5 minutes, cook time: 0 minutes; Serves 1

Ingredients

- 2 pinch black pepper
- 2 pinch ginger
- 1 tbsp honey
- 2 pinch turmeric

Instructions

1. Mix all the Ingredients in a small bowl
2. Lick slowly from a spoon over a 10-minute period.

Nutrition Facts Per Serving

Calories 169, Total Fat 24 g, Total Carbs 31 g, Protein 10 g, Fiber 13 g.

Chapter-8 Ayurvedic Recipes for Condiments, Spreads, and Sauces

Fennel Bulb Pesto

A simple, highly nutritional and low-calorie side dish that goes with any dish.

Prep time: 5 minutes, cook time: 10 minutes; Serves 4

Ingredients

- 1 tsp apple cider vinegar
- 1/2 cup chopped cilantro
- 1/2 cup fennel stalk
- 1/4 cup olive oil
- 1/2 cup pumpkin seeds
- 1/2 tsp salt

Instructions

1. Place all the Ingredients in a food processor and blend to make a puree of the desired consistency.
2. Serve with rice or pasta.

Nutrition Facts Per Serving

Calories 15, Total Fat 4 g, Total Carbs 5 g, Protein 2 g, Fiber 0 to 1 g.

Coconut Chutney

Recommended as a high-fat side dish rich in MCTs for keto dieters.

Prep time: 10 minutes, cook time: 5 minutes; Serves 4

Ingredients

- 1 cup coconut flakes
- 1/2 cup chopped mint
- 1/2 tsp sugar
- 2 pinch salt
- 1/4 cup of water
- 1 tsp mustard seeds
- 1 tsp coconut oil

Instructions

1. Add all Ingredients except coconut oil and mustard seeds to a food processor and blend to make a thick paste called chutney.
2. Roast the mustard seeds in coconut oil till the seeds begin to pop. Sprinkle it over the chutney.

Nutrition Facts Per Serving

Calories 15, Total Fat 6 g, Total Carbs 3 g, Protein 1 to 2 g, Fiber 0 to 1 g.

Cranberry Sauce with Ginger

A healthy alternative to the store-bought jams and spreads for your sandwiches.

Prep time: 5 minutes, cook time: 60 minutes; Serves 5

Ingredients

- 1/2 whole oranges
- 1/4 tsp orange zest
- 12 oz cranberry
- 1/4-inch ginger
- 3 tbsp sugar
- 1 cup of water

Instructions

1. Juice the oranges and chop the zest.
2. Mix all Ingredients in water.
3. Bring to a boil. Lower the heat and simmer until it has a jam-like consistency.

Nutrition Facts Per Serving

Calories 25, Total Fat 8 g, Total Carbs 12 g, Protein 2 g, Fiber 0 to 1 g.

Potato Salad with Yogurt Sauce

Makes up for a great dip for your French fries. Can also be used as a healthy spread on burgers.

Prep time: 15 minutes, cook time: 35 minutes; Serves 4

Ingredients

- 4 whole potatoes
- 1 tsp salt
- 1/2 cup chopped cilantro
- 1 tsp cumin
- 1/2 cup chopped mint
- 1 cup of water
- 1 cup yogurt

Instructions

1. Boil potatoes with salt until tender 2 to 3 hours before serving. Let it cool in the refrigerator.
2. Meanwhile, add remaining Ingredients to a blender to make a puree.
3. Pour it over boiled potatoes just before serving.

Nutrition Facts Per Serving

Calories 45, Total Fat 14 g, Total Carbs 15 g, Protein 12 g, Fiber 8 g.

Ginger Lemon Salad Dressing

Suitable to be used as a salad dressing for a keto diet.

Prep time: 10 minutes, cook time: 0 minutes; Serves 4

Ingredients

- 1 lb red leaf lettuce
- 1 lb endive
- 1 pinch black pepper
- 1/2-inch ginger
- 1 tsp honey
- 1 whole lemon
- 2 tbsp olive oil
- 1 tbsp water

Instructions

1. Coarsely chop the greens and place them in a large bowl.
2. Mix the remaining Ingredients in a small cup and pour it over the greens. Toss well to distribute the flavors.

Nutrition Facts Per Serving

Calories 25, Total Fat 14 g, Total Carbs 18 g, Protein 5 g, Fiber 9 g.

Pumpkin Sauce

This pasta sauce contains complex carbs that are suitable for keto dieters as well as people trying to lose weight.

Prep time: 5 minutes, cook time: 5 minutes; Serves 4

Ingredients

- 2 pinch cardamom
- 2 pinch cinnamon
- 1 pinch cloves
- 2 pinch nutmeg
- 2 tbsp olive oil
- 1 cup pumpkin, cubed
- 1 tsp sugar
- 2 pinch salt
- 1/2 cup of water

Instructions

1. Mix all Ingredients and warm it on the stove for 2 to 3 minutes or until the desired temperature is reached.
2. Serve with pasta

Nutrition Facts Per Serving

Calories 35, Total Fat 10 g, Total Carbs 15 g, Protein 15 g, Fiber 8 g.

Cilantro Lime Salsa

This low-calorie salsa recipe is healthy and suitable for weight loss and a vegan diet.

Prep time: 5 minutes, cook time: 0 minutes; Serves 4

Ingredients

- 1/2 cup chopped cilantro
- 1/2 cup chopped red onion
- 1 whole lime

Instructions

1. Chop the cilantro and raw onions. Mix well.
2. Marinate them in the lime juice for 30 minutes.

Nutrition Facts Per Serving

Calories 14, Total Fat 3 g, Total Carbs 4 g, Protein 2 g, Fiber 0 to 1 g.

Plum Sauce with Rosemary

Goes well with sandwiches, pasta, burgers, and fries. Contains complex carbs that are suitable for paleo, vegan and keto diet.

Prep time: 0 minutes, cook time: 120 minutes; Serves 4

Ingredients

- 3 cloves garlic
- 1 tsp rosemary
- 10 prunes
- 10 whole dried apricot
- 1/4 tsp black pepper
- 1/2 tsp salt
- 1 tbsp olive oil
- 2 cups of water
- 1 tbsp white vinegar

Instructions

1. Chop garlic and rosemary and halve the prunes and apricots.
2. Mix all Ingredients in a pot and simmer for 40 to 50 minutes.
3. Mash it once in a while with a potato masher.
4. Continue simmering for another hour.

Nutrition Facts Per Serving

Calories 20, Total Fat 8 g, Total Carbs 10 g, Protein 6 g, Fiber 1 to 2 g.

Chapter-9 Conclusion

Ayurveda believes that our overall health is the outcome of the interconnectedness between the elements occurring within our emotional, physical, and spiritual being. Hence, to stay healthy, a harmony between the thoughts, feelings, desires, emotions, and physical actions must be created.

Herbal medications and other Ayurvedic therapies and practices like Yoga, meditation, massage, and detoxification would help you achieve and maintain this balance, thus promoting optimum health.

Also, your mental, physical, and mental health, which determine how happy and successful you can become in your life depend on the food you eat. It also depends on whether or not you have managed to avoid the factors that harm your health.

If you succeed in making proper changes in your diet and lifestyle, you will find a significant improvement in your health and life in general.

CPSIA information can be obtained
at www.ICGtesting.com
Printed in the USA
LVHW062133050421
683513LV00003B/45